The
Phoenix
& Her
Orchids

Alianna Cabello

Acknowledgments

for my **husband** who pushes
me beyond my limits &
acknowledges my potential
like no one ever has

for my **kids** who i will always
strive to be better for, you
make me whole

for my **mom** who has been
through the ringer with me, i
love you no less

for my **dad** who left this
world too soon, i miss you
everyday

for my **sister** who never judges
me, who lets me simply be me

for my **brothers** without whom,
the world is too big

for **all my readers**
do not be afraid to confront
your

trauma

this is a *trauma* read

as much as it is a *healing* read too

CONTENTS

THE PHOENIX & HER ORCHIDS

I.

Grief

you cannot force
a flower to grow
before its time

you cannot
rob it of its innocence
& expect it to flourish

you cannot grow orchids
in an environment
like this

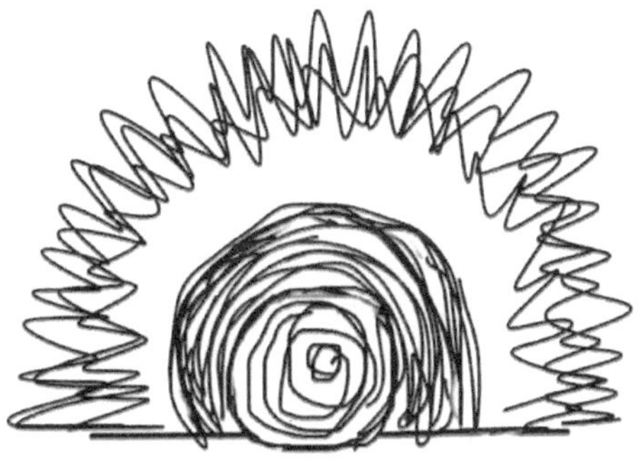

seven-year-olds should stay

seven till the sun

comes back around

& says they are eight

seven is when i lost:
- hair ties
- brothers
- m y s a n i t y

grief will take

a five-minute

smoke break

then turn around

bang on your door

& tell you to let him in

he will disappear

after his knuckles

begin to bleed

then show back up

in two days' time

to repeat the process

all over again

    -   how long will you avoid your *grief*

it does not feel fair

for you to give him eight years

on this earth

& only one year

to know *me*

    -   there was never enough time

does it make my love

for my brother

insignificant

if i cannot

remember us

before he *died*

if i cannot

recollect

memory

after

memory

that i wish to hold so dear

i make visits to graves

to have good conversation

& lay down flowers

on a ground that will not budge

i rid of memories

that haunt my dreams

so i do not have to think

of all that i have *lost*

- what does it mean to grieve

pools are meant to be swam in

but i can no longer

dip myself in

without thinking of him

july is meant for fireworks

but every burst of light

only reminds me of death

we trust it to give life

forgetting it has the power

to take life too

-    water can be so cruel

i h e a r d
my father scream
as he pulled his body
out of our backyard pool

i w a t c h e d
my mom give air
waiting to
receive air in return

i h e l d
my breathe
thinking time would
stop
with it

i c r i e d
alone

there were not enough tears

to go around

& my parents needed

all they could get

- how do i recover

when we could not find him

i blamed myself

for not keeping better watch

for not making him a priority

but i was *seven*

i did not understand

what it meant

to be lost

with no way

    to be *found*

we all blamed

ourselves

for a death

the universe

threw at us

without warning

     - why did we not blame
        the universe

the newspaper

printed his story

& mentioned us

as *survivors*

i hated that

the only thing

we were busy

surviving

was our grief

& how our ways of healing

clashed with each other's

till we became ignorant

of the bottomless void

that slowly consumed us all

when my brother died

he took a piece of our mother

along the way

he took the piece of her

that was not afraid of this world

& left her with unfamiliarity

but she held onto what was left

& held on tighter to her children

whom she could not bare

to let slip through her fingers

all over again

on the worst of days

grief feels like a broken record

& on the best of them

it feels like a strong love

that will go on forever

even *after* death

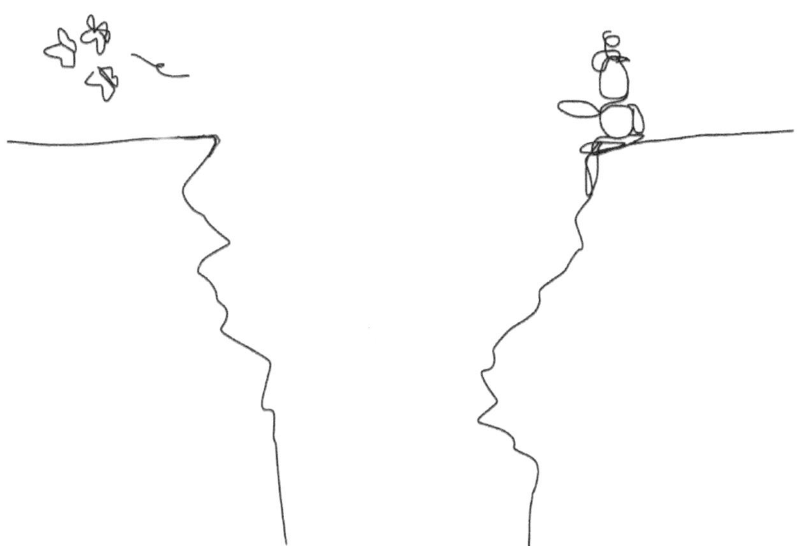

you cannot run

from your grief

for it is like

the wind

always around

      even when you

      cannot see it

i am not sure

what i need

at a time like this

so i will take

all that you can give

& try to carry it all

home with me

while i still

my shaking hands

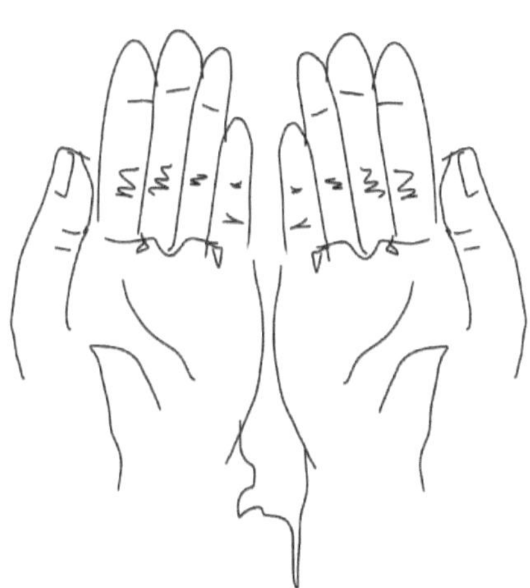

when my brother died

my father ran as far

as his feet could take him

from his family & the promises

he had made to them

my father could never

find enough purpose

in a daughter

who could never

pass on his last name

like a son knew how to do

he tells me to dream big
then tells me my dreams
are not *big enough*

he skips out on quality time
then takes me on roadtrips
to make up for his absence

he lies like it is his living
& always forgets to call

but then he laughs
a hearty laughter
that reminds us
there is good inside him

       – if only he was *consistent*

if only she could

resurrect the ones she lost

but her magic lies dormant

& can only be used

to save herself

- a phoenix dwells inside her

he is the wave

that tries to pull me to sea

to reunite for memories

if only he could catch me

he is the man on the moon

that rocks in his chair

letting me know

he is always there

 - he will be with you
    wherever you go

i search for you

in people & places

& all other things

in this world

that remind me of you

& remind me

that i was a sister

before i knew

what it meant to

grieve

he is with you

when you cry

he is with you

each time you lie

when you tell yourself

you are fine

he rubs your back

& wishes

you could hear him

tell you

it is alright

-    *if i lost you, i would lie to
     myself too,* he says

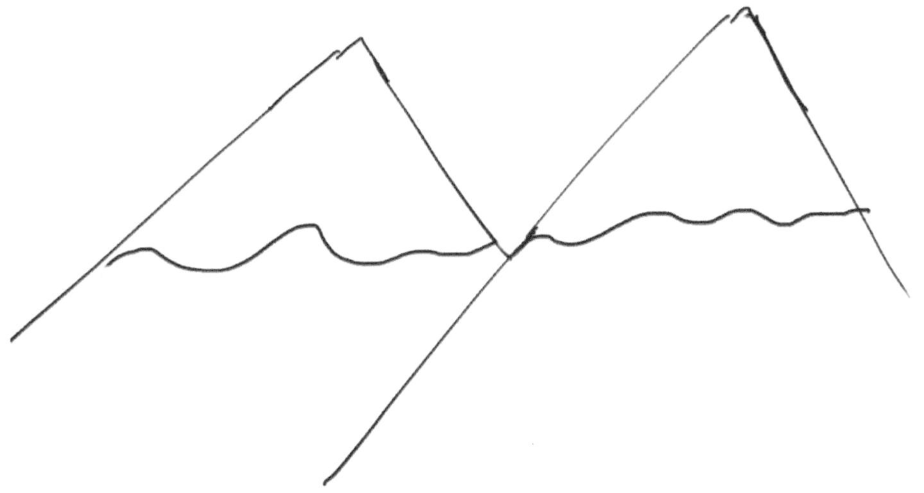

when i die i do not want to be

concealed in a box

underneath the ground

i want to scour the earth

for its highest peaks

& trace myself along its ridges

   -   i want to be free

the saddest people

smile the most

through their pains

& create laughter

out of the traumas

they refuse to dwell upon

i never give my soul a chance

to truly feel the absence

of their presence

maybe it has something to do

with denial

& the way it keeps me afloat

    -   maybe it has something to do
       with *loss*

II.

Abuse

no matter how

hard she tried

she could not

grow her

beloved orchids

in her mother's garden

    – start from *scratch*

some days

i live up

to her expectations

other days

i am the asshole

she accused me

of being

last wednesday

<u>my mother</u>

wraps her arms around me

& kisses me on the head

to keep me from

<u>running away</u>

you will not leave here

without sprinkling some magic

in my garden, she says

i watched my mom

go from deep navy blue

to midnight black

        to flaming red

        right back down to

        a cool minty green

\-   bipolar disease

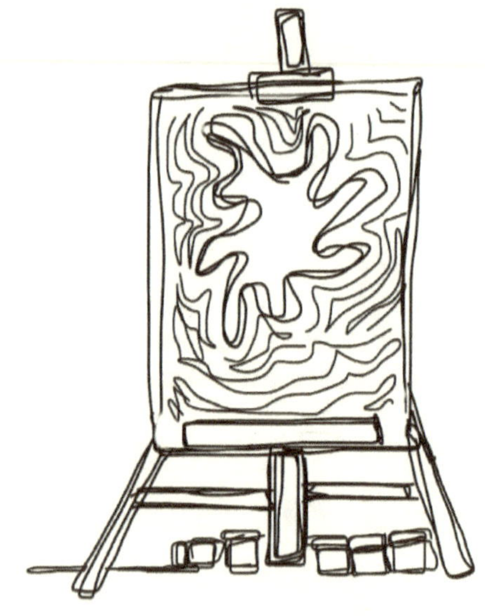

her words hurt

more than her fists

hitting my face

- sticks and stones

she says my touch

is like gold

but there's not enough

gold in the world

to feel like i am *enough*

she says

i never give her problems

but she does not know

i am just scared

to fight back

it is not fair to place

burden upon burden

on a little girl's shoulders

as if they are weights

& she is a well renowned champion

waiting to meet

her *match*

o   avid writer
o   vocal singer
o   happy

-   what i wanted to be
    when i grew up

•   a medical expert
•   law school graduate
•   a realist

    -   what my father
        wanted me to be

i pretend it does not hurt

each time my father

forgets about me

so he can go on thinking

i am the tough child

the one who does not cry

when he is. not there

    - i can do without a love like *this*

i settle for his absence

while his next child

only knows pure love

                    -   i have my
                        own love to
                        live on now

my father feels like a foreign entity

every time he comes around

for he does not know me

anymore than i know him

it does not stop us

from trying to fuse the wires

back together to mend the

broken *connection*

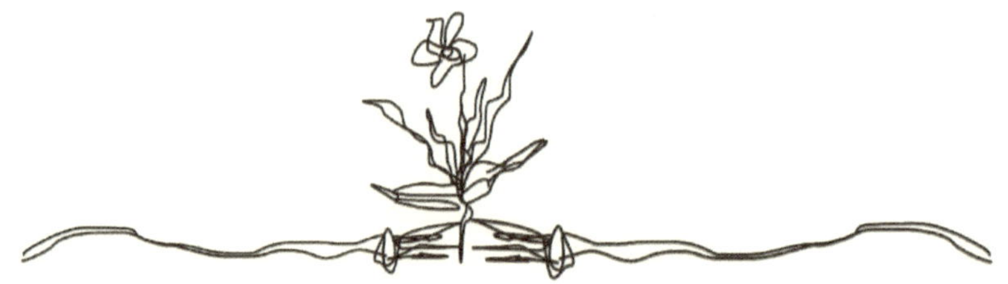

the universe

gives chance after chance

to souls like my dad

who are addicted

to tiny clear bottles

that help them forget

they are in pain

50

an empty bottle

is still a bottle

once full

    - he will drink until his heart
       feels *content*

one day

he will have used up

all of his graces

with the universe

& i will be forced to

revisit my grief

for old times sake

when you look at my *dad*

i h o p e

 you look beyond what makes him human

& see him for what makes him *good*

i h o p e

you look past the bottles

& see a man who loved his family

even when they were less than deserving

i h o p e

you sit him next to our boys

& let him feel the peace & joy

he could never find here on earth

–　a conversation
with the universe

make every moment count

with those you love

tomorrow is never promised

-   advice from a grieving
    daughter

my father's family

tried to plant seeds

they believed

would grow into *gold*

but gold won't grow

if it is talked down to

& seeds won't sew

without *love*

- take care of your garden
  & gold will grow

they reminded the seeds

of all they lacked

& doubted them

each time they grew

but the seeds

knew how to thrive

in their happiness

something their family

could not do

\-   you may be rich but are you *happy*

your garden may not be able to grow
gold

but it is full of love & devotion

that will help your orchids bloom

- note-to-self

my mother's heart tried its best

to fight through all the stress

that tried to seep its way in

in times of failure

it sought help from doctors

to beat much stronger

in order to persevere

her heart

became bigger

to make room

for all the shoes

she had to fill

     -   going it alone is not easy

i learned how easily

my mother got angry

& what kind of

daughter to be

to not feel her *wrath*

     •   maybe i should have been a
        fighter

o   folding towels
o   cooking good meals
o   confrontation

-   all things i am terrible at

•   cleaning
•   not putting up a fight
•   staying quiet

-   all things my mother
    appreciates about me

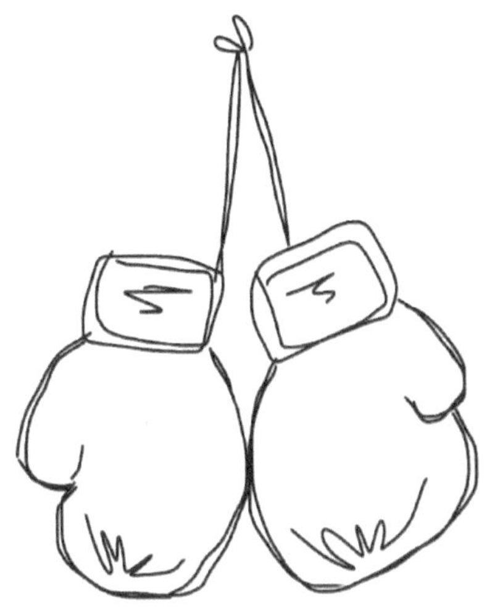

every time my mother got sick

i justified the cage she put me in

she had many battles to fight

& sometimes i fought them for her

- my gloves are hand-me-downs

i grieve for the lost child

that resides within me

with no chance of reaching

the light that is

overshadowed constantly

she tried to rid me
of the defiance
that stirred
inside my soul

in fear it might
burst out
like a raging dragon
& set the world on fire

but i am not a dragon
i am a fucking phoenix

she grew my hair
when she prayed
for it while
she massaged
oils through its
jet black strands

she grew my hair
she declared

then one afternoon
she took scissors
& *cut it away*

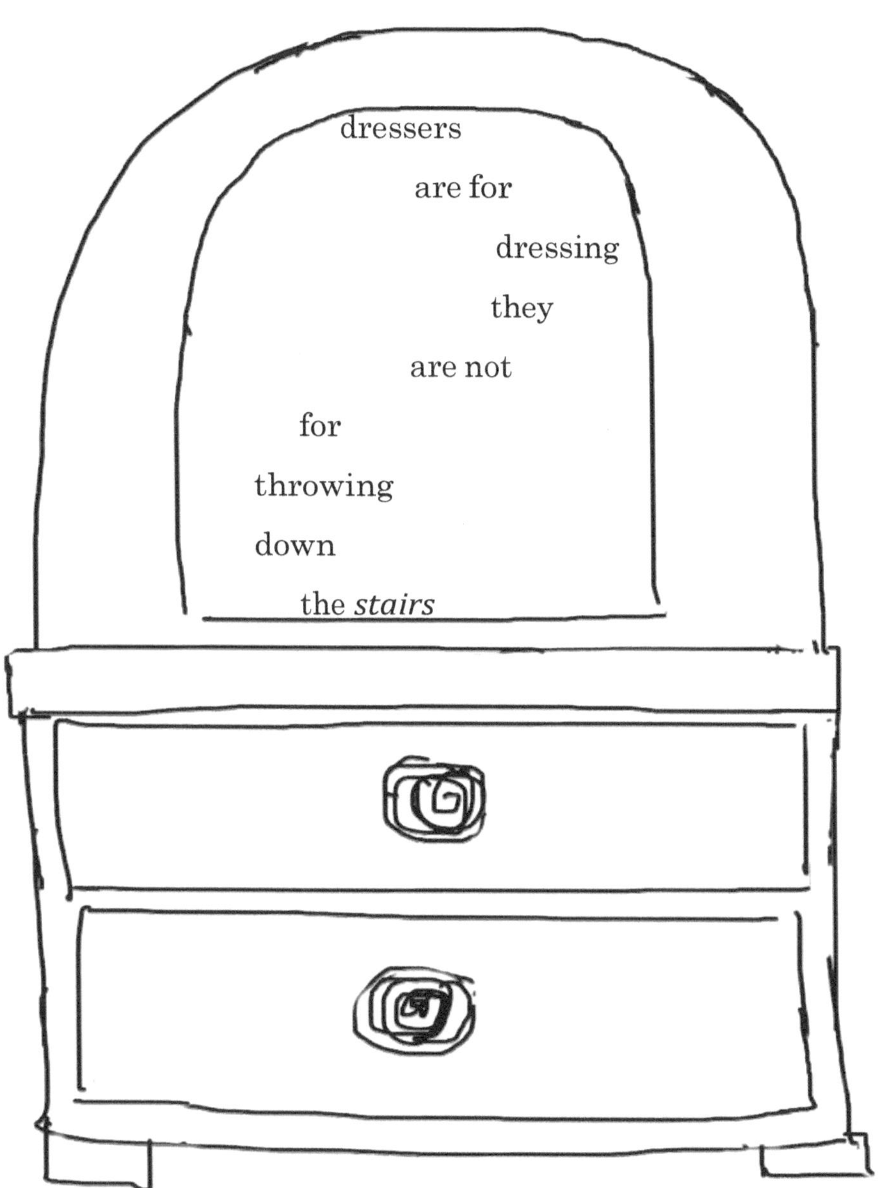
dressers
are for
dressing
they
are not
for
throwing
down
the *stairs*

i prayed to god

to help me

& he told me

he was not giving me

anymore than I could handle

- i am his strongest warrior

i never fought back

my silence protected me

if only it protected her too

there was a time

when she needed me

more than i needed her

    -   sisters protect sisters

it must have been hard for her

to always be in my shadow

as hard as it was for me

to be centered in lights

& displayed like a trophy

locked away in a case

she has always been

the stronger sister

the sister who can

        hold her ground

the sister

who makes sure

i can hold

        my own ground too

we walked on stilts

& tripped over

each other's feet

blaming one another

for our transgressions

　　　　　never stopping to wonder

　　　　　　why the hell we were

　　　　　　　walking on stilts

　　　　　　　　in the first place

　　　-　our life is a circus act

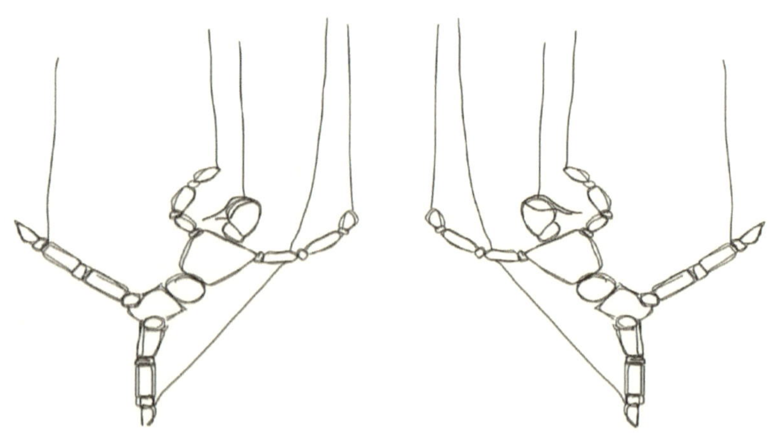

sisters should   not move

across the world   from one another

for she will be missed indefinitely for her

talks & hugs & for her infinite companionship

she is my keeper as i am hers she is laughter

when i cannot find it she is radiant even

when she cannot see it for herself

she does not judge me for the

person i was nor the

woman i have be-

-come

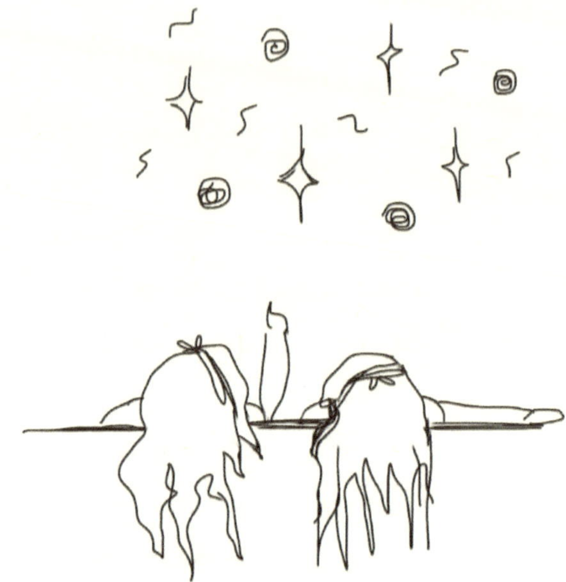

every time we meet

we heal pieces of each other

we never knew needed healing

-    she knows me like
     the back of her hands

an eviction notice

sent us back to a place

full of loss

& indefinitely empty

in body & spirit

- an eviction sent us *home*

when we turned on the pipes

they became flooded with black

& when we tried to find heat

our cold breath became our

company

-     we lived in a home but still
    felt homeless

i watched my mom

beg family

till we looked like

a charity case

no one could be

bothered

to donate to

my mother was pushed away

in her most vulnerable state

maybe that is why

she did not want to return

once she figured out

how to survive on her *own*

they may not have meant

to pour salt in her wounds

but you cannot

do what they did

& use an excuse

like that to *justify* it

being left behind

by those you love

can ignite grudges

that burn for lifetimes

i thought

support was support

even when business

is left unfinished

on the battlefield

        when the cannons

            are loaded

        & ready to be fired

that is when

we are supposed to

drop the act

& remember how much

we love one another

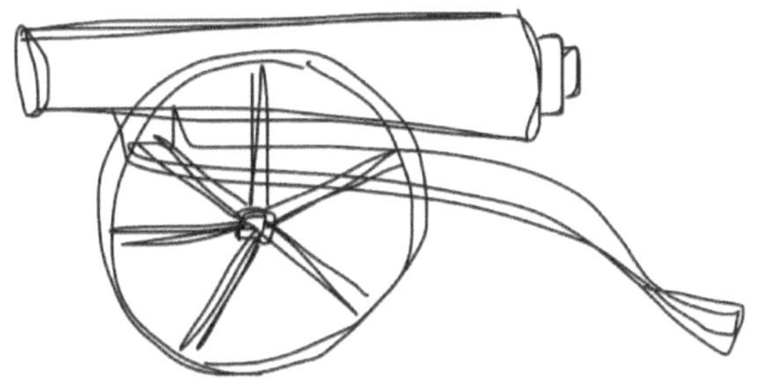

how can i have a family

as big as mine

& always feel

so *distant*

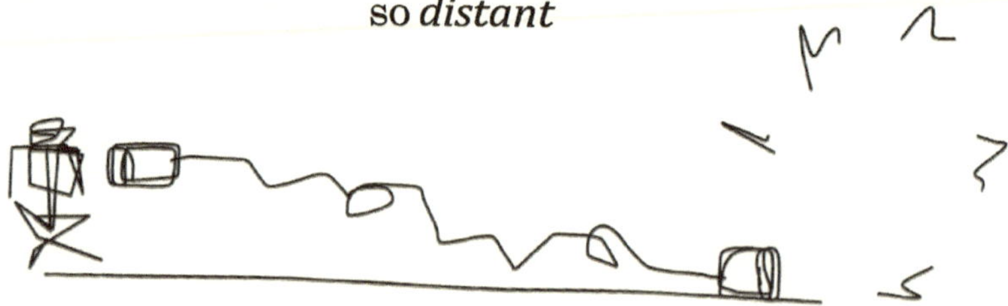

how do i rid myself of trauma

without

turning everyone i love

into villains

she is just a mother

who was trying

to rid herself of a pain

that consumed us all

-     we are more
      alike than you
      think

she is still my mom

in all her pain

& wrongdoings

& i am still a daughter

who loves her mom

despite it all

- we are *still* healing

there were times

when we were happy

she stopped trying

to control the world

& we took a moment

to let out the breath

we had been holding in

for much *too long*

-    we smiled a bit more
     those days

when I was 14

i found outlets in those

who offered any

means of e s c a p e

he was a blessing

to a girl so patient

in a world that constantly

let her down

then he became love too

because he knew

her favorite bible verses

only a saint could recite them all

- even predators read the bible

he made waiting

for marriage

sound like a dream

then continued to touch me

in all the other places

he thought

would not count

as *rape*

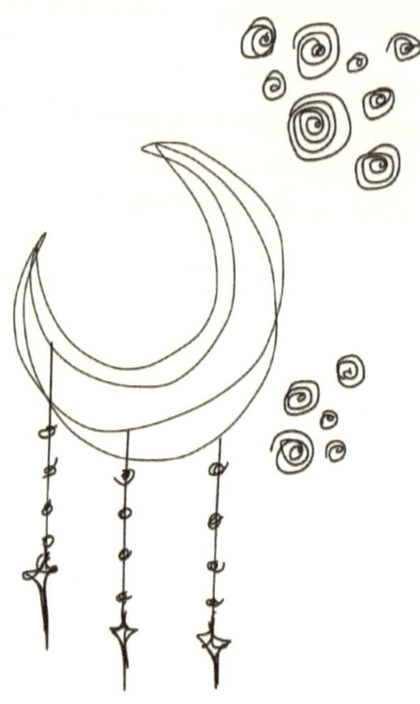

he called me delusional

till i became delirious

with the lies he told

like a bedtime story

he used to lull me to sleep

two years is a long time

- to wait for him to change
- to cry over broken promises
- to keep convincing myself
- ignorance is fucking bliss

- 20-year-old men should not be in love with 14-year-old girls

if you love me

unconditionally

you cannot leave

no matter my faults

or how disgusted

i make you feel

about yourself

you cannot regret me

or rid yourself of my presence

you cannot defy me

    -   *are you sure you love*
        me that much, he says

i do not love you
enough to let you
take anymore of me

i need to spend time
picking up
the pieces that are left
so i can lock them away
for *eternity*

- *i do not think i do,* she says

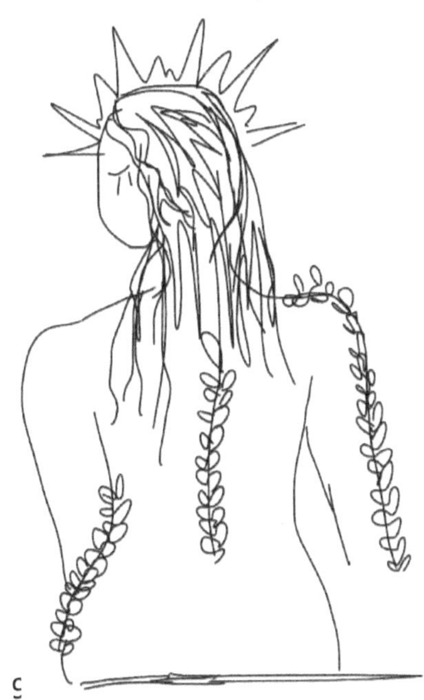

it is difficult to confront

a b u s e

when abusers refuse to take

a c c o u n t a b i l i t y

for the damage they inflict

i want to pick up my pieces

& arrange them into

a work of extraordinary art

never seen before

but how can i create art for myself

when you are in my ear

telling me how to fucking paint

    -   how would you know
          where my pieces go

the world reaches out to me

waiting for my touch

but you live through me

so i cannot see

what i could be

for *me*

   -   when did i become a vessel

i planted seeds into soil

& helped them nourish & grow

spoke love unto them

& watched their gardens overflow

pieces of me given to them

even the pieces i did not know

the more i come to terms

with my trauma

the more memories

become unlocked

& remind me why

i locked them up

in the *first* place

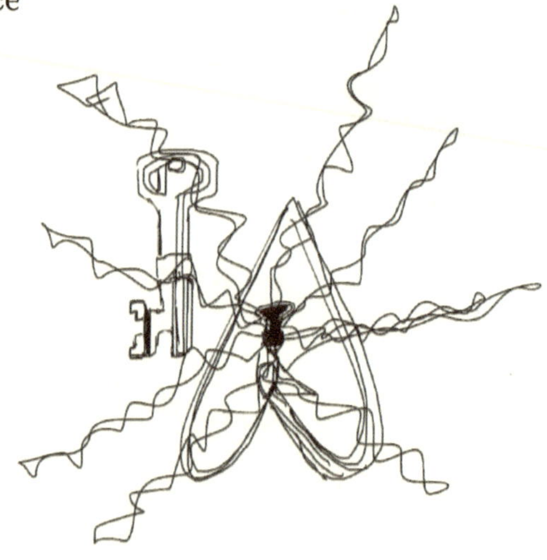

we carry our mothers'

passions & detriments

around with us from birth

not realizing

that the path we are walking

is not our own

it is up to us

to create something new

& set all the best things in *stone*

-    epigenetics

all i ever wanted

was for someone

to be proud of me

it is no wonder

my love language

are the words

i have rarely heard

-   words of affirmation

you can tell me

we had good memories

you can swear it up & down

till your lungs give out

but children remember

what they see

children remember

bad memories

i know good exists within me

when i begin to feel guilty

for putting my trauma

down on paper

i want my trauma

to tell its own story

instead of making me

carry it around

to all kinds of places

it is not *welcome*

you do not have to be

sorry for things that are not

your fault

-    a lesson the
     phoenix still had
     not learned

her scarlet feathers

swayed down to the floor

but she did not fret for she knew she

would be reborn one day

into something much bigger

than she had yet imagined

& something more magical

than anything her parents

had given her

III.

Pain & Pleasure

when i opened up

to the world

is when i felt

most rejected

by those i loved most

my perfection had faded

& my gold washed away

to reveal my copper tones

& tiny hints of grey

my mother told me

i became tarnished

no longer worthy

of display

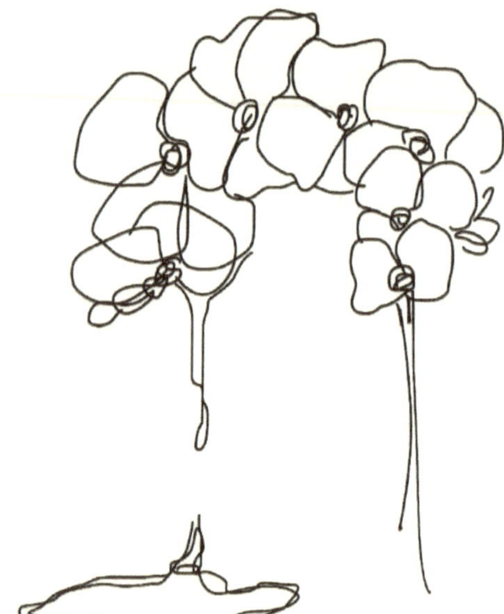

when I was 18

i found solace

in those

who looked at me

& not t h r o u g h me

she was there to watch me blossom

& i was there as she did the same

she was like a sister

so close we were bonded

like two strong roots

entwined with one another

when she cried i did too

& when we laughed

it felt like the universe knew

our match could not be remade

to all my soul *sisters*

when I waited for your call
you were waiting for mine
when you needed a woman
to lift you up
i needed a woman
to carry me through

when we lost touch
i thought you had forgotten me
but watering a garden alone
is hard work
how could i forget

i should have
brought over my watering can
& we could have watered together
filling our gardens with conversation
that would make them grow *greener*

-     women need women

once she spread her fiery wings

she thought her troubles were *over*

no one told her how big

the world could be

& how dangerous it was to explore it

i am afraid

of finding comfort

in the things

that bring me peace

- pain still lingers
where pleasure
blooms

i am the fire

your parents tell you

not to play with

no matter how much

your body craves my heat

but how could you resist

something so tempting

without a little *self control*

in another life

i would have loved you

beyond compare

& engulfed you with my fires

just for standing so near

he let himself listen

to her intoxicating voice

even if the tales were true

& she was like a siren

he would let her

be his *destruction*

i hope i left the most

bitter-sweet

taste on his lips

a taste

he would never

know how to recreate

it is in my blood

to become attached

& when someone leaves

a piece of me

goes with

them

i had to let go of the idea

of what we could have been

that was nothing but a *whisper*

- even that felt easier
  than letting you go

we are two parallel lines

in the universe

——————————————————

no matter how close

we are to each other

——————————————————

we

    will

        never

           meet

it comforts me

that the image of you

no longer wraps itself

around my brain

not even

in the subconscious

of my dreams

do you reside with me

-   it has taken me forever to
    erase your trace

<u>women</u>

do not allow

men

to tell us

what we are

made for

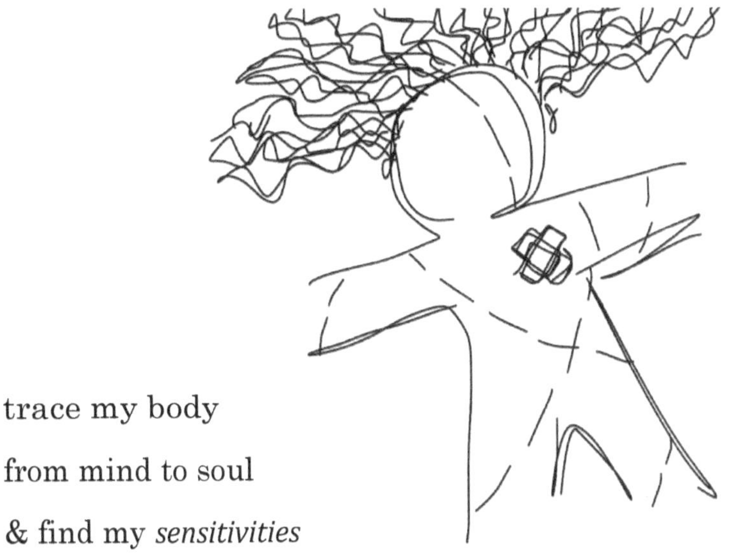

trace my body

from mind to soul

& find my *sensitivities*

spread

out

along me

like a *treasure map*

\-   mind body soul

it is easier to keep my daggers in

than to pull them out

with no one but myself

to stitch my wounds

   -   maybe i should have been a *doctor*

as vulnerable as you may feel

in times like this

you must believe

that you will become

ten times stronger

for the times to come after

- have you
  forgotten
  who you are

do not put so much trust

in others to lead the way

only you are aware of your path

& only you will be able to take it

   -    your path is paved
            for *only you* to see

i am tired of

following people

step

    after

        step

       day

   after

day

just to realize

we are going in circles

\-   do not be afraid to walk
    on your own

you cannot

send out

invitations

to a destination

that is only

meant for you

-    let *yourself* take
     your own journey

i worked so hard

to earn a four year degree

that was supposed to

tell me who i would be

instead it reminded me

of all the things i could *not* be

- listen to your gut

o   lifelong friends
o   a chance to find myself
o   my soul mate

-   the pros of college

•   years' worth of debt
•   no fucking clue how to use my degree
•   migraines

    -   the cons of college

what is for you

will wait for *you*

even through

your impatience

-    you will find your purpose

do not get

comfortable

in the stillness of

today when tomorrow

there is always something new

-    dreams change everyday

you can be good

at something

& still decide

it is not

your cup of tea

it may taste

a little sweet

but there is still

not enough sugar in it

for you to feel satisfied

fuel needs a spark to ignite its fire

i used what is left of mine

to brush through my tangled hair

& force a smile onto my face

making small conversation

i do not bother to remember

for the rest of the day

just to slip right back into bed

& do it all over again

- depression is *depressing*

how long

will you let yourself

run on autopilot

-    take yourself back

i see my dad in me

in pictures & mirrors

& spontaneous addictions

we *love* to pour our pains into

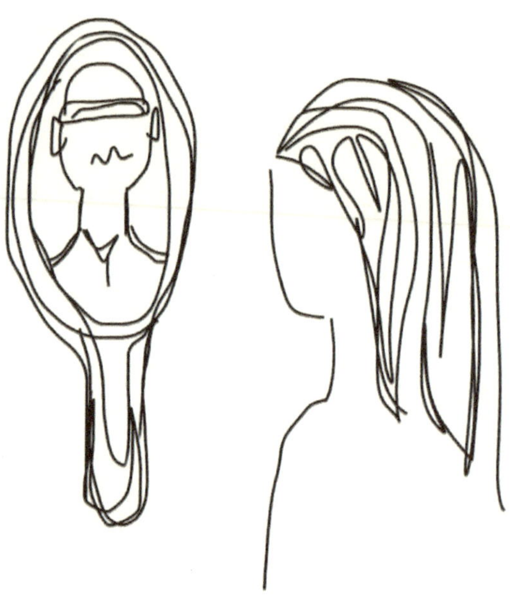

i pry weeds

from their

nesting space

& use my fingertips

to set them on fire

i watch

as they burn

& turn into ash

that loves to

pile at my feet

& when the smoke

finally fills my lungs

i let my guard down

& feel everything

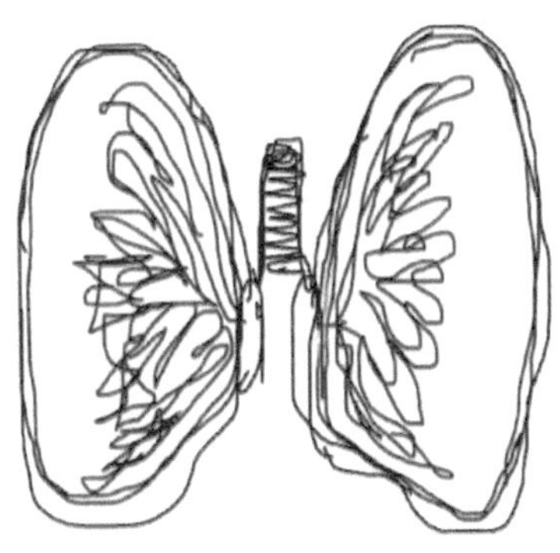

i am as strong as my dad

when he picks the bottle up

& tries to put it down

i am as bold as him too

when he hides the bottle

he recently drank up

& forgets that all liquor

smells the same when you talk

-    it is a battle of the strongest

how come you run

when things start to get better

not everything that is good for you

will feel like silk across your skin

sometimes good things

feel like thorns in your side

yelling at you through your pain

to wake the hell up

- a wake up call for the phoenix

it is alright

to miss the place

you have spent

most of your life

running from

on most days

i miss new york

but on saturdays

i blame it for my problems

-    the source of my problems is

     home

i am still healing

from things

i never speak about

i am still forgiving

for things

they never speak *aloud*

IV.

Love

to the boy

who showed me

that love is *kind*

thank you

for taking your time with me

& for letting my fires burn bright

i appreciate

that you loved me

for my oranges & yellows too

you were the spark i needed

to keep my fires going those days

- thank you for loving me

the phoenix had never

met a man who

did not fear

her magic

- he saw her potential
  & loved her for it

his love filled

her cup till her

cup runneth over

as she outgrew the parts of herself

she did not know anymore

she hoped he would too

she hoped he would look at her

new feathers

& love them as much as her old ones

but the love they had

was built on a foundation

stuck in its ways

& it was because of this she

could not stay

he fights to change her mind

but can never change it

he tries to hate her

but his heart refuses to

for it is filled with

too much love for her

hating her would feel

like an utter

betrayal

- how could he blame
  her for being the
  woman he loves

letting you go

is not an easy thing

for me to do

-   *believe me when i say it,*
    she says to him

when the phoenix

gave up on love

the universe

picked up her heart

& threw it back her way

with a force that left a bruise

in all the right places

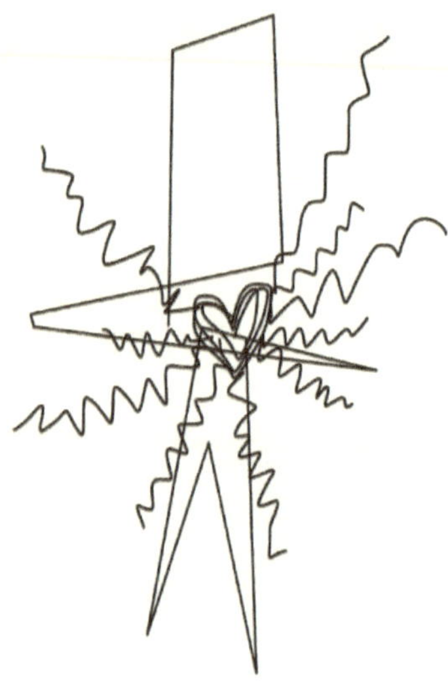

my soul knew

i would love again

so i made sure

my soul remembered

how to love itself first

i am the red ember

he needs to keep himself warm

       he is the cool blue i need

       to quench my thirst

but i am afraid of becoming

magenta purple through his touch

& i am afraid of a love

beyond *return*

the phoenix was afraid

to give love a second chance

but this time around

it felt safe to let her guard down

for someone who understood her

like no one ever could

-    the phoenix felt at *home*

meeting him
felt like a breath
of fresh air

i was drowning
he pulled me up
& gave me
mouth-to-mouth
until i spewed
petal upon petal
all over the ground

his eyes looked through me
& created a window to my soul
that allowed him a glimpse
at all my wonders
i kept hidden from others

i knew then

that the stars aligned

just for *us*

he learned me

& did not hesitate

to sink deeper

within me

-   i am his discovery

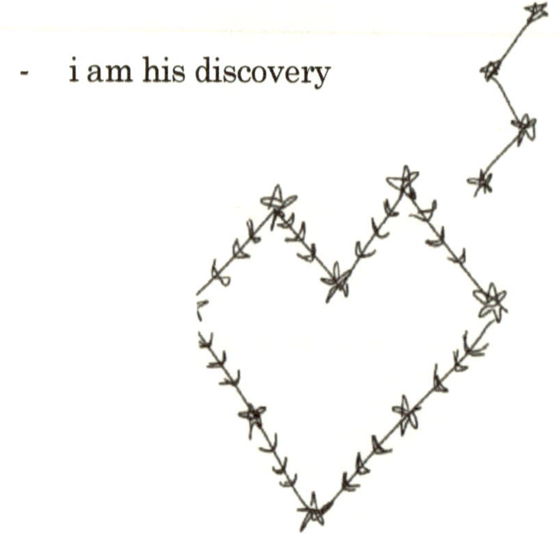

you make me want to

scratch all my plans

& rewrite them with you

i took his last name & told myself that

i would love him till the end

he fueled my fires

& never made me

extinguish them

& when he gazed

upon my gardens

he added fertilizer

instead of stealing

orchids

he told me my garden was vibrant

& he was not surprised

that others had stolen from it

but he would be there always

to keep it *safe*

- i think we both found each
  other at the right time

it is like we are on

the same train of thought

& we get off at the same stop

why would i be there

without you he says

so much of my childhood

was robbed in my sleep

so i give to my daughter

the good parts of me

so her childhood can breathe

for my childhood

resuscitates within me

through watching her

be able to be

as she should be

i heal

her knee scars

with kisses

& heal

my dormant scars too

i tell her

she is fierce

& remind myself

i am too

& when she yells

i love you mom

i yell louder

    i love you too

she is more him than me

in the way she sees the world

as her oyster

& knows that one day

she will find her pearl

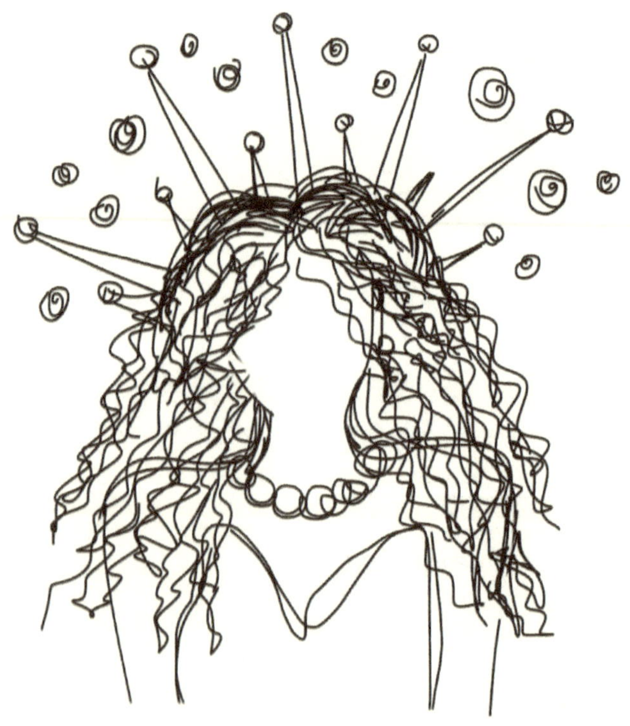

before my ribs began to ache
from the kicking of your feet
you were loved

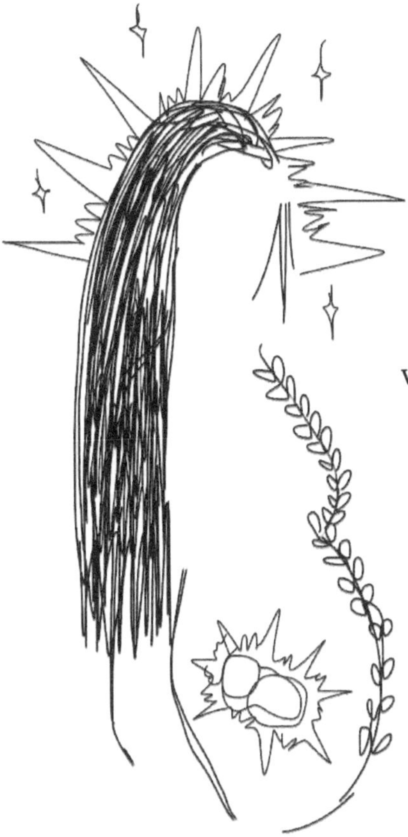

before you ever
spoke the
words mama
& knew
what it meant to say
the words
i love you
you were so loved

you were loved
as an idea
& much more
for all the times
to come after

\- if you should ever wonder

she radiates a love

whole enough

to share with others

like honeybees

unaware of their

own mark in the world

but if your energy

throws her off

even for a second

she will not hesitate

to let her sting

subdue you

-   my little bee

we named her after

the princess

because we knew

she would grow into

the general one day

-    my daughter, leia

the dark scares me

more than it does her

but i will light our way

so she can see the things

i was never able to see

      -   i am a mother
           covered in trauma
           wounds pt I

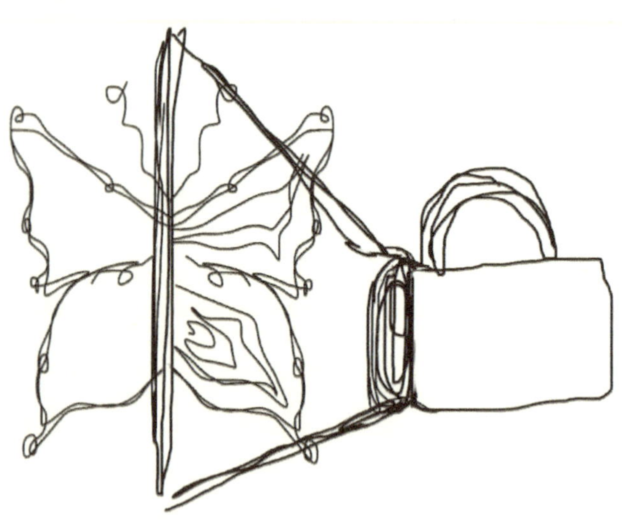

i am trying not

to hold on so tight

that i stop her

from becoming

who she is meant to be

- i am a mother
  covered in trauma
  wounds pt II

i am a realist

i will not sugarcoat

this world to you because i have seen

what it can do

but I will make sure

you know love

beyond compare

& i will fill your mind

with enough knowledge

to make you feel prepared

rather than afraid

of the life that waits

to be explored by you

-   i am a mother
    covered in trauma
    wounds pt III

my daughter is almost

the same age as my brother

before the universe

gave up on him

i have to make sure

she knows

i would never

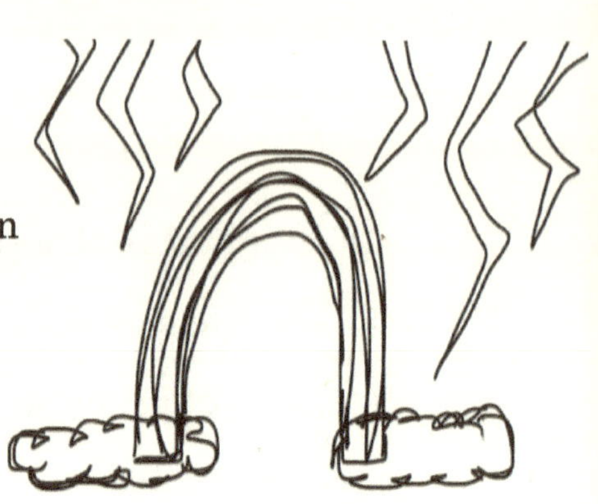

i wanted to create
more life in our garden
made from love
but my flowers
wilted instead

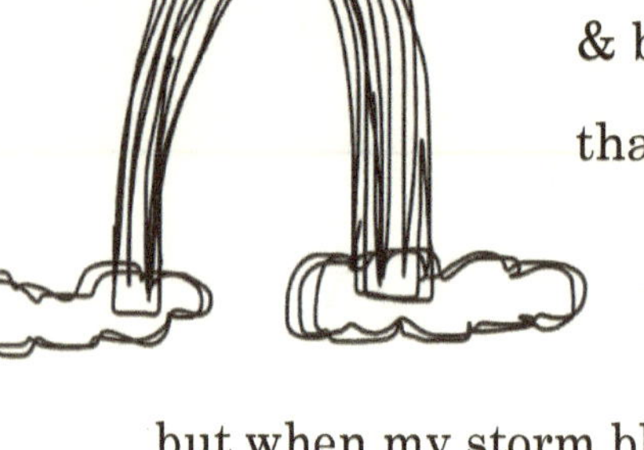

i cried till my tears
became monsoons
& brought thunder
that shook the trees

but when my storm blew over
rainbows took its place
-    you cannot mask
what you took,
I yelled to the skies

i

felt

  betrayed

by

  my own

body

& i could not help

but see a *monster*

every time i

looked in the

mirror

-    1 in 4 pregnancies
     result in
     miscarriages

i never knew motherhood

could bring so much joy

yet so much *sadness* too

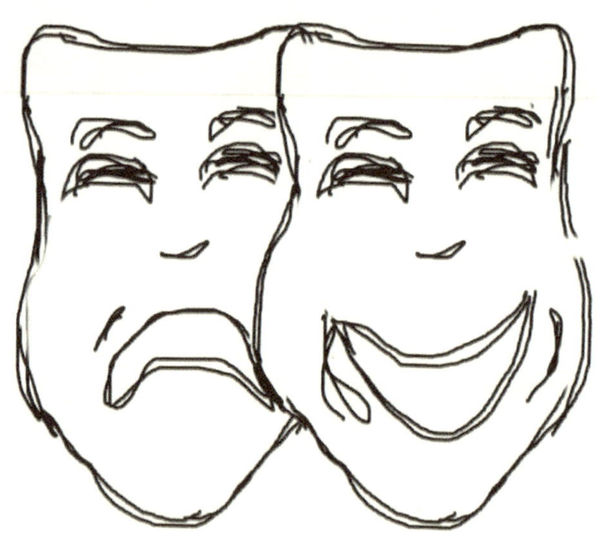

i keep holding onto this idea

that the man i married

will come home

one of these days

to realize that my effort

was far from good enough

after losing something so *dear*

he does not see the faults i see

he looks at me & sees

the woman he married

the dreamer & the lover

the kick-ass warrior princess

she just has her

guard up again

& that is *okay*

- you are so loved

if i ever caught a glimpse

of our future

i would see us

in all our *joy*

when he is gone

& i am too

i hope our children

spread our ashes

in all the same places

so we can travel the world

all over again

till we are reincarnated

through love

- our love makes me believe in soulmates

love is not to be perfected

for it is controlled by

forces strong enough

to make you stumble over

even when you try to balance out

V.

Healing

you are a phoenix

rise up from your ash

\-   you were *made* for this

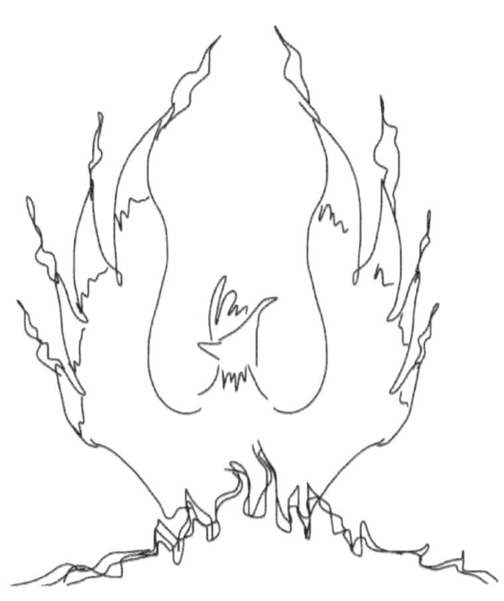

at some point

i stopped forcing myself

unto this world

& let it crash into me

for a change

these claws

belong to you

you can choose

to clip them

or accept them

for what they are

-    come out to play

the woman in the mirror

looks back at me

& promises

to keep me afloat

this time around

she looks like

she has seen

her fill of the world

i come from a line of women

who never rely

on the validations of

others to take the

journeys

we intend to take

-    my origins pt I

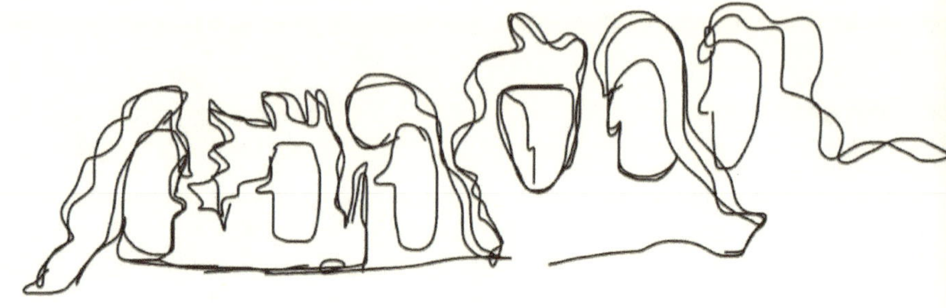

i come from a line of

women that take the word

mana

to heart but still struggle

to understand what it is

to lean on each other

in times of need

to accept what is different

& embrace what stays the same

-    my origins pt II

i come from a line of women

that sweep their traumas

under the rug

while they ignore their pains

& create generational patterns

sewn into us

from mother to daughter

like scratchy knitted sweaters we

wear to make her happy

-   my origins pt III

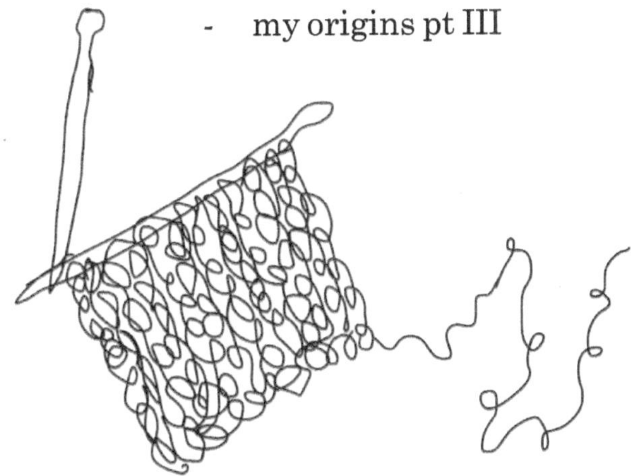

184

i will no longer sacrifice

myself at the expense of

scratchy sweaters

185

i am tired

of consuming

all my darkness

so their feelings

remain intact

stop holding it all in

till you become

a time bomb

for those who never

see it coming

-    scream your truth out

this is my truth

it is ready to be understood

as if it is a lost language

& must be reintroduced

into the world

stop using duct tape

to put yourself

together again

you are complex

find something that can fit

into your intricate pieces

& reunite them

like never before

let me fill all your cracks

with *gold*

let me show you how to perform

kintsugi

i could not remember

how to stay quiet

after I found

my voice

these branches

tangle around me

& into each other

i took a pair of shears

& set myself free

i tried to set you free

from your

comfortability

but you are not ready

to see outside your trees

so i let you be

but still i must

cut the branches for me

-   i outgrew you

your apology

came too late

i hope you did not

expect me

to wait around

for you

to decide whether

i deserved one or not

- if i wanted to wait on
you, you would have
met me in a diner

to forgive

is to let go

of grudges

sworn to be kept

till the ends of time

do not let

your pain

consume you

        -    forgiving is for *you*, not them

people will kick you to the ground

so they can use your shoulders

to give them boosts

then tell you it is still not enough

-    take back your power pt I

they will take from you

till you can give no more

then ask for your

arms & legs too

   -   take back your power pt II

do not let them

intimidate you

for you are a phoenix

& they are house sparrows

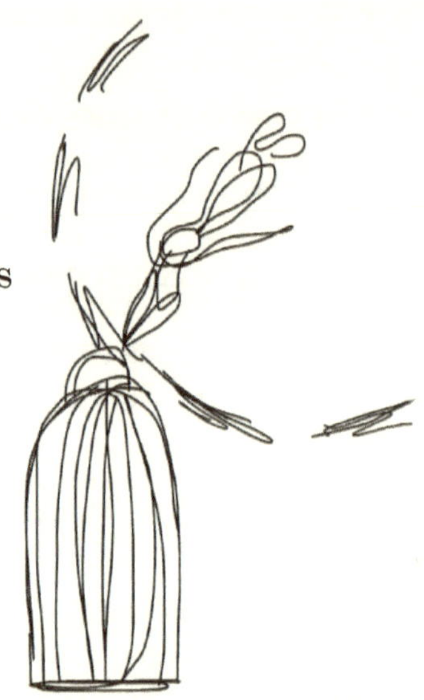

it is time you realize

how much power

lies dormant

in your hands

let the sparrows go

they are weighing

you

down

-   take back your power pt III

you are running

a marathon

against yourself

because

i never saw you

as competition

-   i can run my own race

i am working with a wound

that has bled for years

i am trying to stitch it

for the tenth time over

trying to rid myself of a dagger

that has outstayed its welcome

i just want to write

all my trauma away

unapologetically

& without hesitation

fuse my words together

to create a symphony

it is not possible

to feel better

when all you do

is run from your pain

do not run phoenix

face your fears

look the monsters

in their face

& tell them to begone

for they have abused

your graciousness

for far too long

it is time

someone gave them

a piece of their mind

    – reclaim who you are

i am sorry for the chaos

i bring with me

i did not mean for it

to become entwined

with you

- a sincere apology to those i have
  been less than *kind* to

i will never be

who you want me to be

for you see

ordinary red

never thinking

there is more to me

than the fire & ash

i have allowed you to see

    -   this is who i am

do not limit

yourself to violets

when you can grow

majestic orchids

plus anything else

you set your mind to

-   grow with your potential

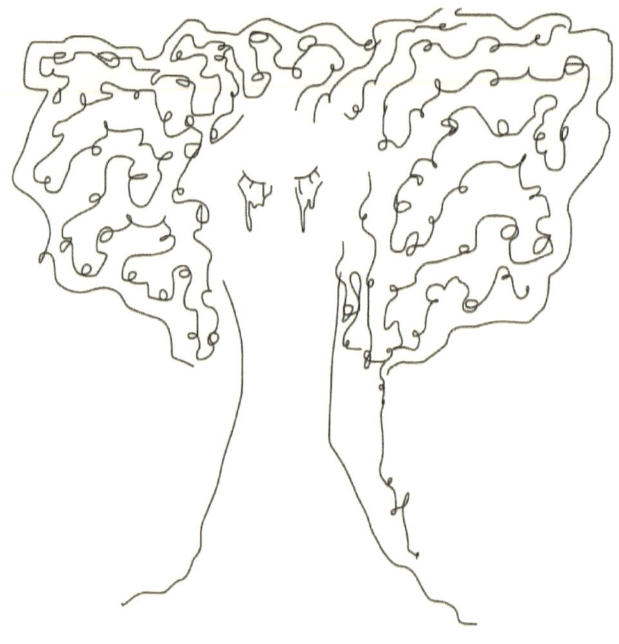

she is mistaken

for the rush of a waterfall

each time she goes by

because of the way

she tries to skip

to the best parts

of what the universe

has set out for *her*

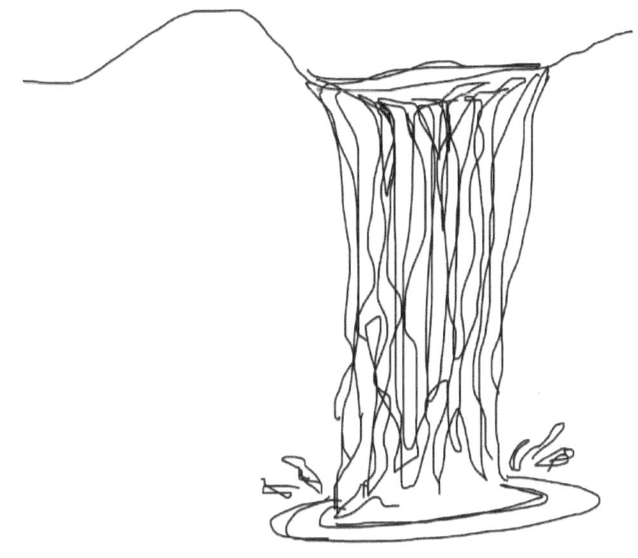

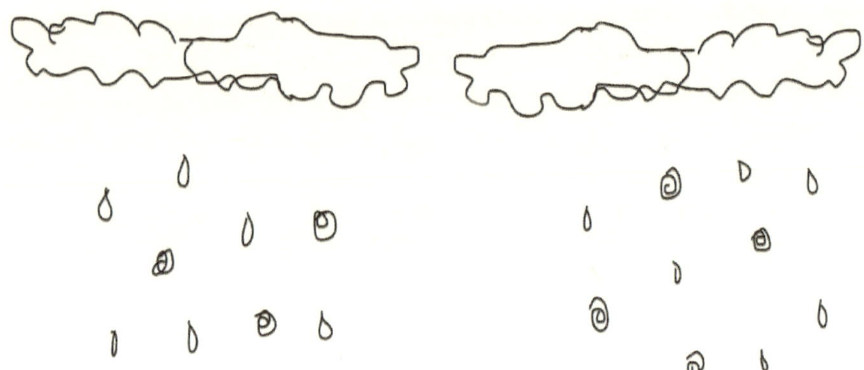

dance in the rain even

if you are soaked

let it water

your gardens into

flourishing greenery

cry while it disguises

your tears & hold yourself tight

& when its droplets turn into

pellets let the rain be your

release

you can handle anything

the present day throws at you

because you survived

everything your past days

forced upon you

october is not afraid to change

it embraces its colors

with a loudness

that lets you know it is here

-   october is a month full of *beginnings*

the phoenix was born

one early october morning her

mother cradled her

in her arms & promised her

the best this life

would have to *offer*

the phoenix was reborn

one late october evening

she cradled herself

& promised herself

she would try again

to find the best of both *worlds*

let yourself ignite

till you explode

& are reborn

from the ash

that overtakes you

    - let your trauma go

with each crimson feather

that shed from her body

a burden fell away

one that always sought comfort

on her *shoulders*

& created so much

turmoil inside her *heart*

i am bright

like the sun

it is not my fault

you cannot handle

my heat

    -   think again before you
        come around me

why would i settle

for meteor showers

when my name is written

in the fucking *stars*

- never settle for less
  than you deserve

self love

is the hardest

form of love

to accept

- it took a long time
  to love myself

i spent so much

of my life

waiting on

the world

to supply my

happiness

           -   i think it is time i create
               my own

every day i have to remind myself

that i no longer need to

keep anyone's garden alive

except my own

      –   it is time to sow my own seeds

the winds have changed direction

& the tides have gone off schedule

for your footprint

makes   the   world   quake

something it cannot handle

this season is yours

do not let it go to waste

this is your moment

do not let anyone

steal it from under you

do not be afraid

to start anew

    -   you are fearless darling

you have made it

to this point

do not give up

on yourself now

your wings will take you

as far as you tell them to

i did not get up one day

& decide to write a book

for sentiment

i did it for me

& the phoenix

that i set free

from her *insecurities*

when i think about what the universe

has lined up for me my eyes

fill with water

& my heart beats a little faster

because this has always

been my *destiny*

her garden grew with her

& from it came hope

for a future

she could not see

but knew would be

waiting for her arrival

–   do not be late to your own party

she wanted to see

how far her wings

could take her

in hopes she could

fly to the moon

& spend some time

up above in the cosmos

where *no one* knows

her name

\-   phoenix, you can do anything

Author's Note

The author would like to note a few things to help the reader better understand her story. Alianna was born into a family of *six* as the second eldest child. Her family consisted of her mother, father, two brothers and one younger sister.

Her eldest brother died during Alianna's first year of life and her youngest brother passed on when she was only seven.

At ten years old, she shockingly discovered that her father whom she grew up with was not her biological father. As you read, you should note how she refers to her paternal father as 'father' and biological father as 'dad'. This note is here to help readers avoid confusion while reading through her journey.

She hopes that readers will enjoy her story enough to stick around to the very *end*.

About The Author

Alianna Cabello is an up-and-coming writer who enjoys writing poetry and fiction as much as she loves reading the two. Currently she resides in Nevada with her husband & kids. She received her BS in criminal justice in 2021 at Liberty University but her passion for writing led her down a different path.

Her focus at the moment is poetry but she plans to transition her focus towards fantasy fiction (a genre she has been eager to explore)! Alianna wrote this book to encourage others & give hope when it seems as if it is nowhere to be found.

She also wanted to share her story to show that perseverance can pull anyone through. This story has no short cuts or sugar-coated sentences. It is simply and chaotically the *truth* and nothing but it.

A big thank you to Dana Alsamsam for taking the time to edit this masterpiece. The first of mine in a long line to come! Find her at danaalsamsam.com.

You can keep up to date with Alianna and her next plans on her social media handle: @aliannacabello on Tik Tok & Instagram.